Wrangell-St. Elias National Park and Preserve

By Nora L. Deans

Alaska Geographic Association
Anchorage, Alaska

Alaska Geographic thanks Wrangell-St. Elias National Park and Preserve for their assistance in developing and reviewing this publication. Alaska Geographic works in partnership with the National Park Service to further public education and appreciation for national parks in Alaska. The publication of books, among other activities, supports and complements the National Park Service mission.

Author: Nora L. Deans

Photography: Bob Adkins, 40-41; Michael Collier, 6, 17, 25; Mark Emery, 23, 30; Bill Hess, 26; © 2007 Franz Lanting/www.lanting.com, cover; Ernest Manewal, 9, 18-19; © 2007 Fred Hirschmann, iv, v, vi-1, 8, 10, 20, 28-29, 32, 42 (raven), 46, 53, 55, 60, 66-67; National Park Service, 12, 48, 63, 27, 33, 58-59, 61; © 2007 Ron Niebrugge/www.wildnatureimages.com, ii-iii, 2-3, 4-5, 7, 14-15, 31, 34, 36, 38-39, 41 insets (whale, ptarmigan) 42-43, 44-45, 49, 52, 56, 62, 64-65; Robert Valarcher, 35;

Other images: Page 24, Fish illustrations courtesy of Canada Department of Fisheries & Oceans, Pacific Region Communications Branch; Page 50, University of Fairbanks, Alaska, Rasmuson Library, Francis Pope Collection, 66-15-723N; Page 51, National Park Service, 1885 engraving of an Ahtna cache and sled from Lt. Henry T. Allen "Report of an Expedition," Plate No. 8; Page 57, Anchorage Museum of History and Art, B52.51.12 Illustrations: Denise Ekstrand

Maps: Courtesy of the National Park Service

Design: Chris Byrd

Editor: Susan Tasaki

Series Editor: Nora L. Deans

Project Coordinator: Lisa Oakley

Agency Coordinators: Vicki Penwell, Tom Vanden Berg, Smitty Parratt, National Park Service

www.alaskageographic.org

Alaska Geographic is the official nonprofit publisher, educator, and supporter of Alaska's parks, forests, and refuges. Connecting people to Alaska's magnificent wildlands is at the core of our mission. A portion of every book sale directly supports educational and interpretive programs at Alaska's public lands. Learn more and become a supporting member at: www.alaskageographic.org

ISBN: 978-0-930931-57-5

Library of Congress Cataloging-in-Publication Data
Deans, Nora L.
Wrangell-St. Elias National Park and Preserve / by Nora L. Deans.
p. cm.
ISBN 0-930931-57-2
1. Wrangell-Saint Elias National Park and Preserve (Alaska)--Description and travel. 2. Natural history--Alaska--Wrangell-Saint Elias National Park and Preserve. 3. Wrangell-Saint Elias National Park and Preserve (Alaska)--History. I. Alaska Natural History Association. II. Title.
F912.W74D43 2007
917.98'30444--dc22
2005030610

Printed in China on recycled paper, using soy based inks.

Crown of the Continent

Contents

A Vast Wilderness

Snowy peaks throw off the mantle of clouds that sometimes cloak this northern landscape. Blackburn, Sanford, Drum and Wrangell: On a sunny day, the mountains beckon from the highway. A vast, rugged wilderness awaits, a heaving, restless, ever-changing landscape across which glaciers surge and calve into the sea, rivers weave braided beds, and steam escapes from a slumbering volcano. From roadside or backcountry, a visit to Wrangell-St. Elias National Park and Preserve takes you back 10,000 years to the Great Ice Age, which spawned massive icefields and glaciers and buried mountains and forests under tons of snow and ice.

For thousands of years, people have explored these isolated lands and coast, yet many mountains, creeks, rivers and glaciers remain uncounted, unnamed. Wilderness still exists here, in a territory larger than six Yellowstones.

Molten lava and flowing ice sculpted the landscape in Wrangell-St. Elias National Park and Preserve, but it's the mighty rivers, the Copper and the Chitina, that set the patterns of life here. Melting glaciers release trickling streams that roar to life, eroding mountains; gorging on glacial silt, trees and boulders; and threatening to carry away those who brave their waters. Icy floes may threaten bridges during breakup, but these rivers also bring life to the land, and to those who dwell here.

For the region's first people, rivers brought salmon, grayling and burbot, and riverbanks became sites for seasonal villages. For explorers, raging water and turbulent currents created barriers too treacherous to cross unless frozen thick in the heart of frigid winters. For prospectors, rivers washed away rock to expose gold. Bush pilots followed silvery threads of water as guiding beacons, and eyed sandbars as makeshift landing strips.

Vast and wild, these rivers and this land invite, yet resist, familiarity. Only two roads pierce the forests and tundra. Some will venture into the heart of the wild anyway, to climb icy peaks, search for wildlife, camp along a remote stream, fish and hunt to feed their families, or explore a ghost town. They seek a true wilderness, mostly untouched, always challenging and humbling, unrestricted and uncontrolled—a place where wildlife roams free across thousands of miles of spruce forest and wetlands, tundra and alpine clearings, and rocky coasts. Here, Dall sheep and mountain goats graze on rocky crags, leaping nimbly from one to another. Herds of caribou migrate along ancestral paths to wintering grounds and harbor seals haul out on ice floes at the feet of calving glaciers.

However, to the first people to inhabit this land, it was never wild, it was never vast, it was just home. The Native people, whose ancestors dwelled here thousands of years ago, hold sacred many places in the park. Their descendents strive to preserve their privacy, stories and homeland. Their lives, like the streams and rivers, are tightly braided into the region's rich history of mining and prospecting.

First proposed for National Park status in 1939, these wild lands had to wait until 1980 and the passage of the Alaska National Interest Lands Conservation Act (ANILCA) to be officially designated as a national park and preserve. More than 13 million acres were carved out of the 100 million-plus set aside for permanent federal protection. From cirque to sea, entire ecosystems are now wilderness, preserve and park on a scale known nowhere else.

4

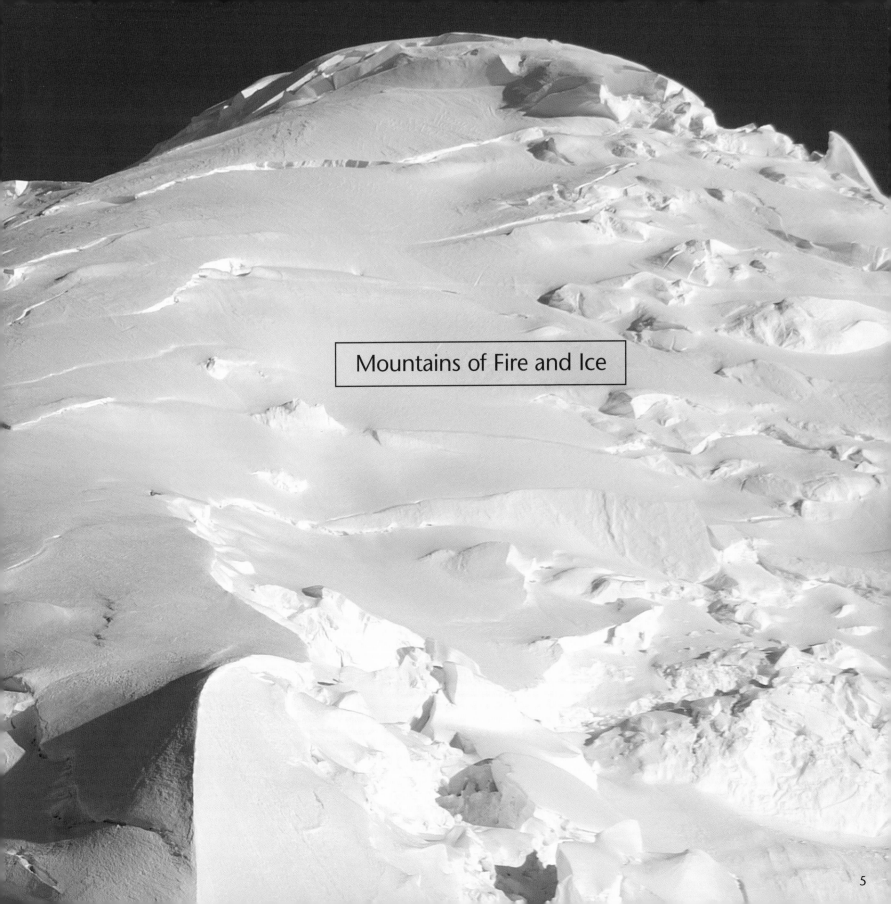

Mountains of Fire and Ice

Rock glaciers only occur where it gets cold enough for water trickling between rocks to freeze and form an ice matrix. Gravity pulls the weathered rock downhill, and the top flows faster, rolling over the front and forming a characteristic slope at the toe.

On this day we sighted land. The land consisted of huge, high, snow-covered mountains.

—Russian Officer Sven Waxell, sailing under Captain-Commander Vitus Bering, on the sighting of Alaska, July 16, 1741

What explorer Vitus Bering and his crew saw in their first glimpse of Alaska was the highest coastal mountain range in the world. They found an icy, rocky wilderness where only the hardiest survived, and tall peaks that rose dramatically from the Gulf of Alaska. Along this southern boundary of today's national park, rugged valleys, glaciers and bays punctuate the landscape, dwarfed by an 18,008-foot-high mountain called *Yahtsetesha* by the Tlingit, and named Mount St. Elias by the early Russian explorers.

More than 200 million years before Vitus Bering's ship crept close to these icy shores, colossal forces began sculpting the landscape, and continue to do so. But the real clues to the region's geologic history lie buried under thick icefields or blankets of volcanic ash, which the erosive powers of the rivers have both revealed and carried away.

Geologists do know that massive plates, part of the Earth's crust, slammed into each other in slow motion here, creating a tapestry of geological formations. Southern Alaska is a hodgepodge of the many landmasses that have collided and merged with one another over the millennia. Where landmasses meet, major faults occur, which makes the region prone to earthquakes. Few will forget the powerful Denali Fault earthquake of 2002.

Sheer walls and glaciers cap the snowy peak of Mount Blackburn.

7

Twenty-six million years ago, as the Pacific Plate pushed under the North American plate, it lifted the continent and violently folded and forced rock ever upward, creating the Chugach Mountains in the southern part of the park. In all, four mountain ranges march through these lands, legacy of the Earth's restless, shifting past. Nine of the highest peaks in North America dominate the park's skyline, from the coastal Chugach Range and the St. Elias Range in the south to the eastern flanks of the Alaska Range that mark the park's northern boundary, known as the Nutzotin and the Mentasta mountains. The volcanic Wrangells rise in the heart of the park.

Volcanoes—Mountains of Fire

As the ocean crust buckled under intense pressure deep beneath the surface, rocks melted into magma, then erupted as lava, building shield volcanoes in what is known today as the Wrangell Volcanic Field. Most of the Wrangells were once gently sloping shield volcanoes capped with large summit craters, called calderas, but wind, rain and ice have worn away the rock and altered their appearance. Mount Wrangell (14,163 feet) last erupted in 1900, and is still very active; steam rises on cold days from this sleeping giant. Mount Churchill in the St. Elias range blew apart in AD 200 and 750, the second-most explosive volcanic eruption in North America in the last 2,000 years. It spewed thick layers of ash over the northeastern part of the park, devastating life for hundreds of thousands of square miles and leaving behind traces—the White River Ash Bed—just under the soil.

The One That Controls the Weather

Eventually, the mountains rose so high that they created their own weather, snagging clouds that released their moisture as rain near the coast, and as immense amounts of snow at higher elevations. Over time, icefields grew and glaciers buried all but the tips of peaks. Even as the mountains grew, erosive winds and massive glaciers —literally, rivers of ice—wore away the rock, altering the landscape yet again.

Glaciers—Mountains of Ice

Icefields and glaciers continue to advance and retreat over 25 percent of the park's landscape, heaving and melting, scraping and scarring rock for more than 5,000 square miles, the greatest concentration of

Glaciers Move Mountains

When snow piles up faster than it melts, the stage is set for a glacier. The snow's weight forces air out of the flakes, compressing them and turning them to ice. Under this immense weight, and pulled by gravity, glaciers flow downhill, scouring and scarring the land along the way. Glaciers move tons of broken rock and debris, which fall out at their feet, or terminal moraines. Long ribbons of eroded rock, called lateral moraines, darken the edges of many glaciers. Where two glaciers come together, lateral moraines meet and create medial moraines, dark streaks through the middle of the icy flow.

The Athabascans refer to Mount Wrangell as K'eltaeni, "one that controls," acknowledging the peak's effect on the weather.

Uplift and Rebound

At the end of the Great Ice Age, numerous glaciers melted away or retreated from within Alaska. Rebound, the rise of the Earth's surface due to loss of ice and snow, is ongoing in coastal Alaska today. Combined with tectonic uplift from crustal plates pushing against each other, the land is rising faster here than anywhere else on Earth. Southeast Alaska is getting higher at a rate of one-and-a-quarter inches per year, compared to the tallest mountains in the world, the Himalayas, which are rising less than one-quarter inch annually.

glaciers anywhere on the continent. Imagine the state of Rhode Island made of ice 2,000 feet thick, flowing out of the St. Elias Mountains between Icy Bay and Yakutat. This is the Bagley Icefield, North America's largest subpolar icefield at 127 miles long and 6 miles wide. This formidable expanse of ice served as a trade route for the region's early inhabitants, who traveled it to the coast to swap obsidian and copper for goods made by the coastal people.

The Bagley gives birth to huge glaciers: Tana, Miles, Hubbard, Guyot and Malaspina. The largest piedmont glacier in North America, the Malaspina bristles with a carpet of trees and plants that grow in the thick silt scraped off the mountains. They'll thrive until the ice melts, or scrapes them away in turn. Farther north, Nabesna, the world's longest interior valley glacier, flows for 75 miles from the Wrangell Icefield high in the mountains.

A maverick, the Hubbard retreats and advances contrary to other glaciers. From its origins in the icefields of the St. Elias Mountains in Canada to its terminus in Disenchantment Bay, Hubbard is the longest and one of the most active tidewater glaciers in America. By the 1700s, it had retreated for miles, creating an expanse of open water at the coastline that lured explorer Alessandro Malaspina into Yakutat Bay in 1791, where, he believed, he would find the Northwest Passage. Ultimately, his hopes were dashed against a wall of ice, and he left behind evidence of his disappointment in the bay's name: Disenchantment.

Recently, Hubbard Glacier has been surging, advancing more than 1,600 feet since 1986. On July 23, 2002, the glacier pushed its terminal moraine against Gilbert Point, damming Russell Fjord for the second time in recent years and creating Russell Lake, the largest

Crowns of the Continent

Mountains in Wrangell-St. Elias National Park and Preserve, and neighboring Kluane National Park in Canada, rank among the tallest in North America. Mounts Wrangell and Sanford loom large in our view because they rise from a relatively low base of 3,200 feet, unlike the Rocky Mountains, which begin from a mile-high base.

McKinley, Denali National Park and Preserve	*20,320 feet*
Logan, Kluane National Park (Canada's tallest)	*19,850 feet*
Citlaltepetl (Orizaba) Mexico	*18,700 feet*
St. Elias, Wrangell-St. Elias/Kluane National Parks	*18,008 feet*
Popocatepetl, Mexico	*17,930 feet*
Foraker, Denali National Park and Preserve	*17,400 feet*
Iztaccihuatl, Mexico	*17,343 feet*
Lucania, Kluane National Park	*17,147 feet*
King, Kluane National Park	*16,971 feet*
Steele, Kluane National Park	*16,644 feet*
Bona, Wrangell-St. Elias National Park and Preserve	*16,550 feet*
Blackburn, Wrangell-St. Elias National Park and Preserve	*16,390 feet*
Kennedy, Kluane National Park	*16,286 feet*
Sanford, Wrangell-St. Elias National Park and Preserve	*16,237 feet*

ice-dammed lake in North America. If it were to reach 130 feet above sea level, it would overflow out the back of the lake into the Situk River drainage, destroying a world-class commercial and subsistence salmon fishery and dramatically changing a portion of the Tongass National Forest. The town of Yakutat on the coast would be threatened as well. During July 2002, Yakutat residents nervously watched as the water climbed higher and higher, to 75 feet above normal. Heavy rains raised the lake's level even more. Suddenly, on August 14, water poured over the dam, and 300,000 cubic feet of water per second raced out at the foot of the glacier, restoring the fjord and scouring a hole 180 feet deep in the bottom of the bay. Glaciologists report that Hubbard Glacier appears to be insensitive to climate, and anticipate that this largest of the calving glaciers will continue to advance.

As glaciers surge, they rip rocks and boulders from the mountains, adding them to the collection of riprap frozen solid into their icy bottoms. Over thousands of years, grinding, slow-moving glaciers carve deep U-shaped valleys through the mountains. Glaciers are unforgiving, scouring everything in their path and creating a fine, powdery silt known as glacial flour. Glacial streams carry tons of this silt into larger rivers, clouding the water and giving it a distinctive milky color. In summer, meltwater from glaciers high in mountain valleys suddenly swells rivers with churning, silt-laden water, surprising those trying to cross what moments before had been a shallow stream on a warm sunny day. During the winter, when glaciers stop melting, rivers flow clear. 🌼

Earthquake!

Measuring 7.9, the largest earthquake to shake the Earth in 2002 rattled the park, triggering landslides in the Wrangells that littered debris fields with boulders the size of houses and displaced land on either side of the fault more than 18 feet (below). The cause of that strike-slip quake? A continental landmass, the Yakutat block, slammed against Alaska, rupturing the Susitna, Denali and Totschunda faults. Miraculously, no one died, but Mentasta and neighboring communities were badly shaken. The force damaged the Tok cutoff and Richardson Higways, making them impassable.

Ammonite Fossil

A tropical ocean swarming with sea life covered the Wrangell Mountains more than 70 million years ago, confirmed by fossils of ancient sea creatures such as ammonites, and relatives of squid, octopus and the chambered nautilus. When the ammonite died, it settled to the ocean floor and became embedded in the sediment. Time and pressure turned the sediment into mud-stone and shale, and, over millions of years, geological forces lifted these rocks into mountain ranges. Now, ammonite fossils can be found 5,000 feet above sea level, on the icy slopes of the Wrangell Mountains, a long way from their beginnings in an ancient sea.

Explorers & Cartographers

Alaskan surveys have never been and never will be easy. Throughout its history, the geographic investigation has been a tale of hardship and suffering and not infrequently of death. Let those who are not personally familiar with the character of the difficulties not judge it too harshly.

    —Alfred Brooks, U.S. Geological Survey Scientist,1906

Alfred Brooks mapped the country from Lynn Canal near Haines, west through the mountains of the St. Elias range, and northward through what is today Wrangell-St. Elias National Park and Preserve. But he wasn't the first to record the terrain.

    In 1885, U.S. Army Lieutenant Henry Allen set out to make the first geographic observations of the western Wrangell Mountains. He and two other men left Nuchek on Prince William Sound in March 1885, guided up the lower Copper River by Eyak men. They canoed up the Copper River until ice forced them to switch to sleds. When it became too hard to move the sleds over soft snow, they abandoned much of their gear. By April, they had reached the mouth of the Chitina River, where they stored their few provisions at Chief Nicolai's Ahtna village of Taral. Reaching the chief's camp on an upper tributary, Allen and his men received food and information about the territory. After returning to Taral, the Allen expedition continued up the Copper River, naming many prominent features and creating maps that later helped prospectors and European settlers.

On this pass with both white and yellow buttercups around me, and snow within a few feet, I sat proud of the grand sight, which no visitor save Ahtna or Tanana had ever seen.

    —Lieutenant Henry T. Allen, U.S. Army Expedition, 1885

    Five years later, Israel Cook (I. C.) Russell became the first U.S. Geological Survey scientist to survey in Alaska. In 1890–1891, he mapped the massive Malaspina Glacier, Yakutat Bay and the Mount St. Elias region, attempting to climb the mountain several times.

Tiny Rock Dweller with a Big Voice

Sharp calls ring out from a nunatak, warning of danger. The source of the piercing cry is a pika, an energetic, base-ball-sized ball of fur with short legs and rounded ears. Picas live in a network of tunnels and dens among rocks in their isolated fortresses, where they spend most of the year harvesting and storing food for the winter. Unlike other animals that winter-over, they don't hibernate. Scientists believe some colonies of picas have been isolated for so long that they may be evolving into distinct subspecies.

Nunataks
Islands of Life in a Sea of Ice

Blinding winds and temperatures of -40°F and below blast glaciers on the Wrangell and St. Elias mountains. The small rocky islands of stone that poke through the ice are called nunataks, or "land place," by the Inuit of the far north.

Hunkering down around small isolated outcrops, some hardy plants and animals manage to cling to life in these wastelands. Canadian scientists studying icefield nunataks have identified over 150 species of lichens, mosses, plants, birds, spiders, moths and butterflies. Even picas, small mammals related to rabbits, find refuge in these rugged surroundings.

Biologists speculate that as ice retreated and the climate warmed at the end of the last ice age, plants and animals spread out from the nunataks, claiming new territories. Nunataks recently exposed by retreating glaciers give scientists a window into the past and allow them to study how species migrate and populate new areas.

Flowing to the Sea

Rivers

While dwarfed by other rivers, the Copper and Chitina bring life to all who dwell in their watersheds. Native people, and later, Russian explorers, navigated these northern waterways long before Europeans explored the Mississippi.

Chitina River, 120 miles long

Copper River, 278 miles long

Columbia River, 1,243 miles long

Yukon River, 1,979 miles long

Mississippi River, 2,340 miles long

Nature is ever at work building and pulling down, creating and destroying, keeping everything whirling and flowing, allowing no rest but in rythmical motion, chasing everything in endless song out of one beautiful form into another.

—John Muir

At the foot of a glacier, a trickle of meltwater emerges and flows over and around ancient rock. Trickle turns to stream, and stream to raging river: Powerful water shapes this land and its residents—fishing villages and larger settlements existed along the waterways of the northern forests, where the harvest of salmon and other fishes meant the difference between life and death, and frozen rivers became highways during the winter months.

As days lengthen and warm, the trickling stream can become a powerful river, carrying sand, rocks, trees, even boulders as it flows through rocky glacial debris. These rivers, carrying large sediment loads, often form a tangled network of bars, channels and islands, braiding the land.

Largest is the Copper, spawned in the Wrangells and meandering along the western boundary of the park before emptying into the Gulf of Alaska at the Copper River Delta, east of Cordova in the Chugach National Forest. Known for its intense concentration of shorebirds—the greatest in the world—the Copper River Delta attracts 14 million birds, including almost the entire western sandpiper and dunlin populations. Here, they rest and feed before going on to nest on the tundra.

On the other side of the Wrangells, 100 miles deep in the valley that separates the Chugach and St. Elias range from the volcanoes, a stream of meltwater becomes the powerful Chitina River, named by the Athabascan people from the words *chiti* (copper) and *na* (river). Many tributaries flow into the Chitina through steep canyons draining mountains in the entire region. The Chitina River Valley has long been a major access route to the southern side of the Wrangells.

Seals on Ice

Harbor seals and their pups lie on ice floes at the foot of glaciers in Icy and Disenchantment bays. Yakutat subsistence hunters worry about the effect of cruise ships, fearing that the commotion and turbulence that accompany the ships' entry into the bays causes the harbor seals to slip off the ice into the water, and possibly into the jaws of predators.

Together, the Copper and Chitina drain 24,200 square miles of 15 trillion gallons of water each year. Where the Chitina joins the Copper, water races downstream at over 380,000 cubic feet per second. Yet every spring, salmon, fat and hardy from years of life at sea, swim upstream against this rushing force, driven against all odds to spawn, playing their age-old role in the cycle of life

From River to Sea and Back

Salmon returning from the sea deposit their eggs in redds—an area chosen by the females for their nests on the gravelly bottom of mountain streams or lakes—bringing a new generation to life. A few salmon may spawn in the main river, but generally, the water flows too fast here for successful hatching. Most chinook spawn in smaller streams and rivers, and sockeye spawn in lakes, like Paxon or Long Lake, where the run may begin in July and spawning lasts from August until as late as February or March. Sockeye travel as far as Tanada Lake, about 250 miles; in the Pacific Northwest, they may swim even farther, 500 to 600 miles up the Snake River.

The male sockeye's distorted jaws and jagged teeth help it defend against rivals. The male also digs the nest, fertilizes the thousands of eggs laid by the female and guards them until he dies weeks later. Both male and female sockeyes eventually die as a result of starvation and because their systems cannot readjust to fresh water after so many years in the sea. But there's a utility to their deaths. Salmon fry feed on their carcasses, as do the tiny bacteria that are meals for plankton, and the mice, mink, foxes, ravens, wolves and bears who roam the banks, while nitrogen and phosphorous leaching from the dead salmon help fertilize streamside plants. The sockeye's return from the sea and subsequent death bring some of the ocean's bounty to the nutrient-poor region.

In spring, little salmon with yolk sacs, called alevins, emerge from the eggs, and those not eaten by other fish or birds burrow into the gravel until they grow larger. In about a month, inch-long sockeye fry emerge from their hiding places and move into larger lakes for a year or two, eating insect larvae and other creatures smaller than themselves. As they get older, they'll work their way down to the mouth of the Copper River, pausing in the Copper River Delta estuary, where fresh and salt water mix. Once they've adjusted to salt water, they swim to sea, running a gauntlet of predators.

Those that survive roam the open sea for two to four years, hundreds of miles from the coast. Some head south, earning the name "left-handed stock." Others head north. At first, they'll catch plankton and smaller fish, but later will grow fat on herring and hooligan, or whatever they can catch.

Of the 3,500 eggs that started out in the redd, only about 1 percent, or 35 salmon, survive to return to the Copper River, where they leap, jump and swim against its fierce currents to get to their stream or lake of birth. How do they find it from far out at sea? Some scientists say it's the smell, or possibly the taste, of their home waters. Others suggest they navigate by the constellations.

A Salmon "Who's Who"

For thousands of years, Copper River salmon, prized for their rich and delicious flavor, have been an invaluable resource for Alaska's indigenous people.

Chinook/King
Oncorhynchus tshawytscha
Prized sport fish; grows to 60 inches.

Coho/Silver
Oncorhynchus kisutch
Late fall migrant; grows to 40 inches.

Sockeye/Red
Oncorhynchus nerka
Most common in Copper River; grows to 33 inches.

Chum/Dog
Oncorhynchus keta
Doesn't usually make it up the Copper River; grows to 40 inches.

Pink/Humpy
Oncorhynchus gorbuscha
Commercial fish hatchery raises 30 million annually; grows to 30 inches.

Steelhead
Oncorhynchus mykiss
Sea-run version of rainbow trout; grows to 44 inches,

However they do it, these living treasures are the responsibility of biologists at Wrangell-St. Elias National Park and Preserve, who manage them using technology as their eyes in the water. According to the park's fisheries biologist, Eric Veach, as salmon enter the river and swim up to Miles Lake, sonar counts each silvery body that flashes by. Then, Alaska Department of Fish and Game biologists, working with the park's biologist, set season limits for vital subsistence, sport and commercial fisheries.

Salmon aren't the only fish in the rivers. Tasty steelhead, Dolly Varden, arctic grayling, burbot and whitefish also thrive in these silty waters. But only salmon, steelhead and some Dolly Varden ride the swift, tumbling currents of the Copper River all the way to the open sea, and battle their way back.

From Cirque to Sea

A rugged, misty, forbidding coast, the park's only shoreline is rarely visited. White specks—ice floes—drift with the currents. Harbor seals, Steller sea lions, sea otters, whales and clouds of seabirds claim this part of the park as their own.

Steller sea lions haul out on rocks to rest as they pass through on their migration south. In Icy Bay, harbor seals bear their young on ice floes, a refuge from predators. Sea otters dive for food in the kelp forests, then wrap themselves in kelp fronds at the surface to ride out waves. Killer whales stalk seals and sea lions, and resident pods feast on salmon returning to spawn. Humpback whales pass by on their way back from Hawaii with their young, and gray whales negotiate the coast as they head south to Baja (like many other Alaskans) in the winter. Wrangell-St. Elias National Park and Preserve is a tangle of habitats and ecosystems threaded by silvery rivers, woven together into a giant tapestry—thousands of miles of mountain, forest, river and coast—intact and uncontrolled by any save the laws of the wild.

When the milky, silt-laden Copper River flows out to the coast, it bleaches the sea a pale blue as river water fans out into the darker, deeper ocean.

Katie John
Putting up Salmon at Batzulnetas

Gaa Nataelde c'a gha yet k'edesdzet snaan, sta' 'iinn hdaghalts'e'de. *I grew up here at "roasted salmon place" and here is where my mother and father lived.*

    —Katie John

Salmon fishing on the upper Copper River has always been part of Katie John's life. Born in 1915 in Batzulnetas (called *Nataelde*, "the roasted salmon place," prior to visits by Allen), Katie grew up as a member of the upper Ahtna—the *Tatl'ahwt'aenn*, or "headwaters people"—of the Upper Copper River. Batzulnetas is on Tanada Creek near its confluence with the Copper River, and was known for its sockeye salmon runs. In *Putting Up Salmon*, Katie John, Molly Galbreath and James Kari describe how the Lieutenant Henry Allen expedition first documented the fishery at Nataelde in early June 1885, when they met people with dip nets waiting for the first salmon of the season to arrive. According to Allen,

> *The natives were hourly expecting the salmon and would frequently go to the small river nearby and put in the dip net. Inspired by their hopes, June 3 was passed in waiting.… Just before leaving, a series of loud shouts was heard, proclaiming the first salmon of the season. It was a rather small silver salmon, which was placed in a conspicuous place on one of the spruce bough teepees, where all visited it with great sighing and glee.*

Katie John learned the ways of the land from her people. As she hunted and fished in the tradition of a subsistence lifestyle within what would become Wrangell-St. Elias National Park and Preserve, she also learned English and worked at the Nabesna Mine.

Concerned about the loss of the traditional knowledge of her people, Katie worked hard throughout her adult life to preserve this knowledge for her children and grandchildren. In the 1980s, she recorded, in her own language, the oral histories and traditions that had been passed on to her by previous generations.

Katie has been a strong advocate for a traditional lifestyle that has "place" as a centerpiece. When the State of Alaska enacted regulations that barred Katie from fishing at Batzulnetas, her family's traditional fishing village on Tanada Creek on the upper Copper River, she filed a legal action that included the federal government as a party to the suit.

After years of complex legal rulings and appeals, Katie John finally won the right to fish at Batzulnetas, thereby preserving a tradition for her children and grandchildren. Each year, young people spend a week at Culture Camp at Batzulnetas to learn tribal ways from elders such as Katie John. Katie's determination and dedication to preserving her culture have made her a champion of subsistence rights for both Native and non-Native rural Alaskans.

These young kids, they don't know how we live. They don't get the chance to learn their own ways.… Pretty soon, all our ways are going to be gone. Us old people are going to pass on and there is going to be nothing left. There'll be nothing. They don't know their own Indian way of life, these young people. They're just going to be lost, that's all.

    —Katie John

Rivers of Life

Rivers flow in all directions from the clustered masses of mountains. They are wild glacial streams, snaking out of moraines and carving canyons through brilliantly colored formations or fractured walls of dark lava...

—William E. Brown, *This Last Treasure: Alaska National Parklands*

A grizzly swipes its paw into the silty river, its curved claws hooking a sockeye salmon fighting its way upstream. Tearing into the fat-rich skin and pink flesh, the bear feasts. Then, casting away the carcass, the bear fishes out another, and another. Birds and other animals pick at the cast-off salmon. In the wild, nothing goes to waste.

Winter and the starving time are not far off. Before digging a den and sleeping off the winter, bears must gain hundreds of pounds. From snowfall to spring, the bear won't eat, living off its body fat. Here in the northern forests and mountains, where life is often about survival of the fattest, rivers are the literal lifeblood for many species.

Bears, wolves, caribou and other animals need more than the rivers to thrive in the harsh north. They cover thousands of acres of wilderness as they hunt, graze, mate and flee from predators. In Wrangell-St. Elias National Park and Preserve, large swaths of coastal rainforest, boreal forest, alpine tundra, bogs, fens and river beds support more kinds and numbers of wildlife than can be found in other national parks. Recent studies revealed that nearly 90 percent of all the plant species that are known to exist in Alaska can be found within the park's boundary. According to National Park Service botanist Mary Beth Cook, the climate, mountains and landforms create a mosaic of unusually high diversity of plant communities for a sub-arctic region.

Tapestry of Habitats

In this rugged landscape, it's the weather—rain, snow, temperature—and the lay of the land that weave life's intricate patterns, from coastal rainforest to icy glacier to high mountain tundra.

On the coast, some of the fiercest and wettest storms in the world lash the St. Elias range, where up to 60 feet of snow may fall in one year. As moist Pacific air hits the high coastal mountains, it creates a maritime climate, one with rather mild winter and summer temperatures, torrential rain or snow, and hurricane-force winds. In the coastal rainforests that hug the shoreline, Sitka spruce, western

Residents of the state with permits can use dip nets or fish wheels to catch salmon. Dip nets have been used by Natives since before recorded time, but the fish wheel was not introduced to the Copper Basin until 1912.

hemlock, berry bushes, devil's club and skunk cabbage drink in this moisture. Sitka deer forage in the muskeg meadows. More than 133 inches of rain may fall on the village of Yakutat on the coast, and over 225 inches of snow transform the landscape each winter.

In the rain shadow on the other side of the mountains lies the Chitina River Valley, between the north side of the Chugach and the south side of the Wrangells. Mild winters and warm, wet summers bathe the boreal forests bordering the river. In wet lowland forests of stunted black spruce, moose browse in sloughs and bogs, shrub thickets, and moist tundra. Trumpeter swans raise their young on its ponds and lakes. The 59-mile-long road to McCarthy wends its way through open lowland and wooded upland forests of white spruce, poplar and aspen. Breaks in the trees offer breathtaking vistas from steep bluffs bordering the emerald-green Chitina valley. Unlike the coast, the community of McCarthy receives only 17 inches of rain a year, and a mere 73 inches of snow.

Farther into the interior, on the north side of the Wrangells, long, biting-cold winters with less snowfall, and short, warmer summers with less rain distinguish the seasons and determine who will survive. The 42-mile-long gravel Nabesna Road winds through lowland tundra; permafrost-laden hills; and valleys blanketed in wet tussocks, dwarf birch, black spruce, shrubs, willow and alder, habitat perfect for moose, caribou, wolves and bear. Average rainfall here is only 10 inches; snowfall, less than 3 feet.

Patterns on the Land

Most of the park lies buried under ice and snow, buffeted by freezing temperatures and snow year-round. Snow algae, casting a red glow on a sunny day, live on minerals and debris and are among a very small number of icefield residents.

Treeless alpine tundra borders the icefields on rocky slopes, and small plants grow in moist clearings littered with patches of snow. From a distance, the tundra looks barren, but up close, flowers, plants, lichens and mosses grow in a colorful carpet, blooming and sowing seeds between snowstorms during the brief summer season. Some

Permafrost

Throughout much of the park, permafrost lies just under the surface of low-lying basins and north-facing slopes. The permanently frozen ground occurs when soils remain frozen for two years or more and can be 100 to 200 feet thick. Permafrost may be within 1 to 10 feet of the surface, resulting in soil that is cold, wet and low in nutrients. Thick moss layers keep it from melting and hikers may find standing water in spring and summer.

plants have clung to life here for a century, threatened only by the Dall sheep or mountain goats that scramble over the rocky crags, grazing on grasses and shrubs.

Moving down the mountains, timberline borders the alpine zone. Patches of stunted black spruce, willows and blueberry shrubs mingle near clearings filled with wildflowers. Below 3,000 feet, upland forests of white and black spruce, aspen, birch, and poplar cover the slopes of the Wrangells. On south-facing slopes, the permafrost lies deeper under the surface, so the soil is able to drain and will support larger trees.

Trumpeter swans, largest of all the swans, nest on ponds, lakes and marshes along rivers during the summer, and migrate to coastal areas as far south as Washington state for the winter.

Wildlife on the Move

Spring comes late in the park. Up in the mountains, melting snow encourages plants to sprout early in the season, and caribou, moose and bear join other animals heading up to eat these fresh spring greens. They often stay at higher elevations through the summer to get away from clouds of swarming flies and mosquitoes.

By fall, animals are on the move again. Some migrate, often long distances, to find warmer weather and food. Birds may migrate all the way to South America, or just head to the coast. Grayling move downstream to deep, unfrozen water for the winter. Caribou also migrate. Three herds—the Nelchina, Mentasta and Chisana—live in the park for at least part of the year. The Nelchina and Mentasta are barren-ground caribou that travel hundreds of miles between their summer and winter ranges. The smaller woodland caribou make up the Chisana herd, which has a smaller range and so doesn't migrate as far.

Caribou (right) graze on the move. During the summer, they leave the forests and head for higher elevations to flee predators and insects. In winter, herds migrate to lowlands, where the snow is not as deep and they can find lichens, their favorite food. While bulls from the Mentasta herd mingle with the Nelchinas at times, the Chisana herd keeps to itself, wintering in the Yukon and summering in the park. Its numbers are small and declining, dropping from 3,000 animals in the 1960s to only 700 today. This prompted biologists in the Yukon Department of Environment to try a captive breeding program, according to wildlife biologist Mason Reid. The National Park Service relies on natural processes and allows populations to fluctuate—they monitor and inventory, but rarely intervene. Off-limits to hunters, these caribou are most vulnerable to wolves, bears, golden eagles and other natural predators during the first two weeks of their lives.

As many as 25 wolf packs roam the park.

Dall sheep, one of Alaska's signature mammals, do not need to migrate; their vertical world provides what they require to survive. More than 25,000 Dall sheep live in the park. Researchers, who use remote sensing to determine habitat and relate the quality of each area to sheep density and horn size, believe that the Dall's numbers are stable in some areas and declining in others. In the southern Wrangells and the Chugach range, mountain goats can sometimes be found living near the sheep.

Survival

Wildlife that stay may hibernate. Ground squirrels line hidden chambers with plants, where they'll sleep through the winter—going without food, water or eliminating wastes, and surviving significant declines in internal temperature. Wood frogs leave their tundra ponds and lakes in the black spruce forests and bury themselves in shallow holes until spring. During hibernation, both experience body temperatures that fall below freezing, but somehow they survive.

Bears fatten up on high-calorie berries and salmon before curling up in dens for long winter naps. They emerge many pounds lighter—as well as hungry—in the spring.

Winter or summer, animals in the park stay out of sight and away from people, except for the occasional snowshoe hare, arctic ground squirrel, or fox that sometimes wanders near roads and trails. These smaller animals may risk human encounters as a way of avoiding their predators, which shy away from populated areas and signs of people.

Bison

Five thousand years ago, the wood bison lived nearby, but habitat change and hunting drove them nearly to extinction. Today, herds of these bison roam Canada, and the Alaska Department of Fish and Game is considering re-introducing them to suitable habitat north of Fairbanks.

Two small groups of introduced Plains bison live in the park's lowland forests: the Copper River herd, which now numbers 110 individuals, started with 17 buffalo introduced to Slana, in the park's northern section, in 1950. These animals gradually made their way south following the Copper River. The Chitina herd started with 35 buffalo, but its numbers remain small; about 40 animals make up this herd today.

Bears

Towering over a person when standing on its hind legs, a 9-foot-tall adult bear may weigh up to 1,500 pounds. The telltale shoulder hump sets the brown grizzly apart from the smaller black bear.

No one knows for sure how many bears live in the park. Biologist Jim Wilder studies the bears in Kennicott Valley around the historic towns of McCarthy and Kennecott and has counted at least 84 black bears and 8 grizzlies. Black bears and the larger grizzlies overlap territories in Wrangell-St. Elias National Park and Preserve, but there are more black bears near McCarthy, and fewer in the north near Nabesna.

Grizzlies eat almost everything, including salmon carcasses that wash up in the fall. Unfortunately, the bears' natural curiosity, along with their excellent sense of smell and constant quest for food, brings them into contact with people. The park recorded 157 conflicts in two years in the McCarthy study area, often involving young male grizzlies, resulting in the deaths of 15 bears during the 2000–2001 season. The park is focusing on educating residents and visitors, providing electric fences, an improved burn-barrel plan, and bear-resistant containers to prevent conflicts and more bear deaths.

Sampling of Species

Alder	*Alnus* spp.
Western hemlock	*Tsuga heterophylla*
Mountain hemlock	*Tsuga mertensiana*
White spruce	*Picea glauca*
Black spruce	*Picea mariana*
Sitka spruce	*Picea sitchensis*
Balsam poplar	*Populus balsamifera*
Birch	*Betula* spp.
Willow	*Salix* spp.
Shrew	*Sorex* sp.
Little brown bat	*Myotis lucifugus*
Arctic ground squirrel	*Spermophilus parryii*
Coyote	*Canis latrans*
Wolf	*Canis lupus*
Red fox	*Vulpes vulpes*
Northern lynx	*Lynx lynx*
River otter	*Lutra canadensis*
Wolverine	*Gulo gulo*
Black bear	*Ursus americanus*
Brown bear	*Ursus arctos*
Moose	*Alces alces*
Barren-ground caribou	*Rangifer tarandus granti*
Woodland caribou	*Rangifer tarandus caribou*
Bison	*Bison bison bison*
Mountain goat	*Oreamnos americanus*
Dall sheep	*Ovis dalli dalli*
Arctic ground squirrel	*Spermophilus parryii*
Red squirrel	*Tamiasciurus hudsonicus*
Beaver	*Castor canadensis*
Northern red-back vole	*Clethrionomys rutilus*
Porcupine	*Erethizon dorsatum*
Collard pika	*Ochotona princeps*
Snowshoe hare	*Lepus americanus*

It takes about three months for a male moose to grow a rack of antlers that may span six feet. They fall off after the mating season, and regrow each spring. Clockwise from top right: hare, red fox, river otter.

Sampling of Species

Sea otter	*Enhydra lutris*
Steller sea lion	*Eumetopias jubatus*
Harbor seal	*Phoca vitulina*
Humpback whale	*Megaptera novaeangliae*
Killer whale	*Orcinus orca*
Canada goose	*Branta canadensis*
Trumpeter swan	*Cygnus buccinator*
Rock ptarmigan	*Lagopus mutus*
Red-throated loon	*Gavia stellata*
Bald eagle	*Haliaeetus leucocephalus*
Red-tailed hawk	*Buteo jamaicensis*
Golden eagle	*Aquila chrysaetos*
Peregrine falcon	*Falco peregrinus*
Kittlitz's murrelet	*Brachyramphus brevirostris*
Northern hawk owl	*Surnia ulula*
Northern flicker	*Coloptes auratus*
Black-billed magpie	*Pika pika*
Common raven	*Corvus corax*
Black-capped chickadee	*Poecile atricapillus*
Wilson's warbler	*Wilsonia pusilla*
Golden-crowned sparrow	*Zonotrichia atricapilla*
Dark-eyed junco	*Junco hyemalis*
Pine grosbeak	*Pinicola enucleator*

Far right, northern hawk owl perches on a tree, scanning for prey. Unlike other owls, hawk owls hunt by day in summer. Clockwise: raven, humpback whale, and ptarmigan.

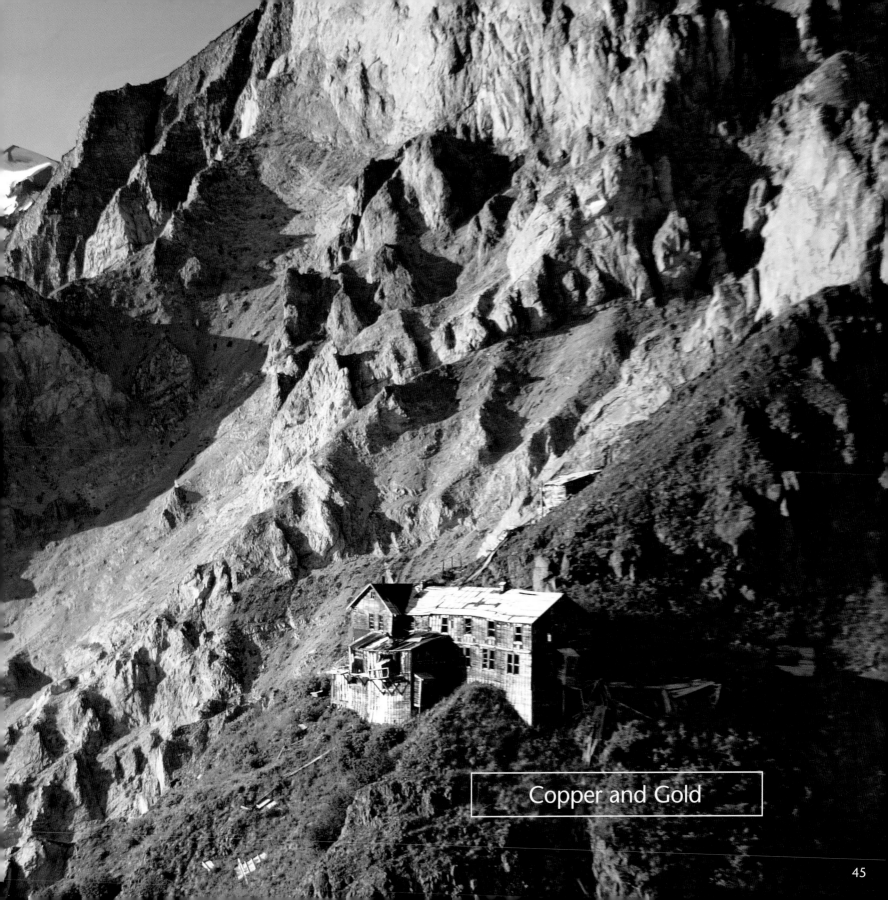

Copper and Gold

Nutka lupine line the rocky shore of the ice-strewn Taan Fjord off of Icy Bay, within 10 miles of the summit of Mount St. Elias.

46

Jack brought his find to my attention. "Mr. Birch," he said, "I've got a mountain of copper up there. There's so much stuff sticking out of the ground that it looks like a green sheep pasture in Ireland, where the sun is shining at its best."

—Stephen Birch, 1900

Native peoples were the first to explore and settle here. Archeological evidence tells a 9,000-year-old story of some of the early human inhabitants of the region, who probably descended from those who crossed over the Bering Land Bridge. As glaciers receded, people ventured farther into the Copper Valley.

From remnants of fire hearths and flakes of obsidian used to make tools, a picture emerges of the Late Denali people, nomads who traveled constantly, hunting caribou, gathering plants, and trading copper and obsidian throughout what would become Alaska. Later, the Northern Archaic people lived in much the same way. Obsidian and copper from the inland region were carried to coastal people as far south as modern-day Vancouver over trade routes crossing the massive Bagley Icefield, and to the east.

Later arrivals, the Northern Athabascan people stayed longer in one place and left behind not only evidence of more permanent, semi-subterranean homes, but the ancestors of the region's modern-day Native citizens. They set up small familial villages where major tributaries entered the Copper River, and moved seasonally for resources. Until the arrival of European explorers changed the region forever, they lived off the land.

The Eyak, who now live in the Copper River Delta, may have first settled the Copper Basin 1,000 years ago. Invading Athabascans later took over the interior of what is now the park, forcing the Eyak south; they themselves were never conquered by Europeans. According to National Park Service historian Geoffrey Bleakley, Russians seeking furs and trade in the 1790s ventured into the interior from the coast; as they traveled, they mapped the land and established footholds, including a trading post southwest of the Copper River Delta, and in 1819, Copper Fort, a trading post near Taral. In the mid-1800s, the Russian American Company sent explorers upriver, but when they took slaves and raped women, they angered the upper Ahtna near Batzulnetas, who massacred the whole party. The Russians never went there again.

In 1867, the United States bought Alaska from the Russians. Visions of gold lured prospectors and explorers north through the Yukon, and some came through Prince William Sound. The first American to reach the mouth of the Chitina River was George Holt in 1882, and the first prospector, John Bremner, wintered in Taral in 1884.

In the late 1800s, miners came north … from Valdez. If it weren't for the Natives' knowledge, they would have all disappeared.
    —Kenneth Johns, Ahtna, Inc.

By the turn of the century, four different Native American groups lived or used resources in what is now Wrangell-St. Elias National Park and Preserve: the Ahtna and Upper Tanana in the northern and interior areas, and the Tlingit and Eyak along the coast. When prospectors first arrived, approximately 1,000 Ahtnas lived along the Copper River.

Fearing clashes with Native residents, and determined to map the territory, the U.S. Army dispatched a series of expeditions that plunged deeper into the Copper River basin and laid the groundwork for future scientific expeditions. Along the way, they met small clans of Ahtna, who were by then wearing western-style clothes and carrying guns, probably acquired through trade with Hudson's Bay Company.

In 1884, Lieutenant William Abercrombie attempted to ascend the Copper River but stopped at the rapids that now bear his name. A year later, Lieutenant Henry T. Allen set out on an arduous, five-month, 1,500-mile-long journey from Prince William Sound through the Interior, ending up at the Bering Sea in September by following the Copper and Chitina rivers. His travels complete for the year, he caught the last boat leaving the Alaska coast before winter freeze-up. Allen, who led the first scientific expedition to cross the Alaska Range from the Gulf of Alaska, named many of the Wrangell Mountains, including Mount Drum, Mount Sanford and Mount Blackburn. He went on to explore the Koyukuk, Tanana and Yukon rivers, creating a legacy of detailed maps and charts.

Abercrombie later traveled from Valdez up the Lowe River Valley and over Thompson Pass. In 1899, he oversaw the building of the Trans-Alaska Military Road, called the Valdez Trail, from Valdez to Eagle. Later, roadhouses sprang up along the trail, often near Ahtna villages; some of these roadhouses eventually grew into sizable communities: Copper Center, Gulkana, Gakona, Chistochina and Slana. Captain Edwin Glenn and Lieutenant Joseph Castner led a team that approached the region from Cook Inlet, following rivers and crossing passes, ending up at the Tanana River. The Glenn–Castner team was the first American group to cross the central Alaska Range.

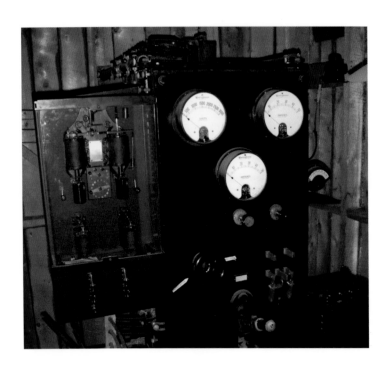

Theft of Artifacts

Cabins, artifacts from Native people or debris from the mining era (above) provide important clues to what life was like here in the past. These things may appear to be trash, but in many cases, are all we have to tell us about the human experience of a place. What's more, under the terms of the Archeological Resources Protection Act of 1986, removal of artifacts and destruction or vandalism to historic structures are illegal, and those who break this law are subject to federal prosecution.

Ahtna people regard the Wrangell Mountains as sacred places. They may have climbed the lower slopes to harvest sheep but limited the amount of time spent there.

50   son   Chief Nichah   Mrs Chief   Mrs Chief "

Chief Nicolai
Traditional Leader

During the last decades of the nineteenth century and until his death in 1902, Chief Nicolai was a powerful leader of the Lower Ahtna peoples. A traditional chief, or *denae*, he enforced tribal law, organized subsistence activities and the redistribution of food, headed trading parties, and negotiated with nearby tribes. A charismatic leader, Nicolai was successful in getting others to work for him, and to respect his leadership.

Chief Nicolai controlled rich fishing sites and major sources of copper from his village at Taral, near the mouth of the Chitina River. He led his people during the time of the early days of American exploration and prospecting and helped the struggling expeditions of Frederick Schwatka in 1891 and Henry Allen in 1895. He also traveled down the Copper River to deal with American traders on Prince William Sound.

In 1899, Chief Nicolai revealed to early prospectors the site of copper outcroppings in the McCarthy Creek drainage, which triggered an explosion of mining in the Wrangell Mountains.

At nine o'clock, we came to the junction of the Chittyna and Copper Rivers.... Nicolai, the chief, was present and gave us a hearty welcome and a still heartier dinner of tea, some dry Graham bread and a great slab of bacon each. It does not seem wondrously palatable just now, looking back at it ... but if I could combine its palatability of that time with its present price in the great cities, I would not exchange the combination for the richest mine in the world.

—Frederick Schwatka, 1891

More and more prospectors poured into the Copper River region, traveling on foot and using simple tools to look for buried "treasure." The worldwide excitement surrounding the Klondike gold discovery in 1896 lured thousands of prospectors to the north in search of instant wealth. Some panned for gold on the tributaries of rivers, while others struck gold lodes near Nabesna and Bremner, or copper near the Kennicott, Chitistone, Kuskulana and Kotsina rivers.

Meanwhile, the U.S. Geological Survey sponsored scientific expeditions into the Chitina Valley, where, on one survey, Oscar Rohn found copper in a glacial river. He named the river and glacier for the late Smithsonian naturalist Robert Kennicott, and McCarthy Creek for prospector James McCarthy.

Rohn's find led prospectors to explore the Kennicott Valley in July 1900. According to Bleakley, Jack ("Tarantula Jack") Smith and Clarence Warner were resting when they spotted a large green "sheep pasture" on the hillside far above. Scrambling up to the spot, they found a fabulously rich copper deposit, which they aptly named "Bonanza." (Over the next forty years, millions of dollars in gold and copper flowed from the region's placer and lode mines.)

The Kennecott Mines

From 1900 to 1902, Stephen Birch, a young mining engineer, purchased a controlling interest in the Bonanza Mine and organized the Alaska Copper and Coal Company to develop it. With financial support from the Guggenheim brothers and J.P. Morgan in the so-called Alaska Syndicate, Birch reorganized in 1905 as the Kennecott Mines Company, which later became the Kennecott Copper Corporation. Some say the confusing spelling, changing "Kennicott" to "Kennecott," was an error, while others consider it to have been deliberate. At any rate, it stuck.

To get the ore to the port at Cordova for shipment to Seattle, and to supply the miners and mill workers in the isolated Kennicott Valley with lumber and other heavy equipment, entrepreneurs built the 196-mile-long Copper River and North Western Railway through impressively inhospitable country. Almost 30 miles of trestles lifted the rails above the nearly impassable terrain.

Gold
Copper was king, but gold was the crown prince of the region. While none of the gold mines, including the Chisana and Bremner, reached the scale of the Bonanza, Whitham's Nabesna Mine produced nearly $2 million worth of gold in the 1930s.

The construction of the "Million Dollar Bridge" over the 1,500-foot wide channel of the Copper River, where it flowed between Miles and Childs glaciers, rivals the building of the Alaska pipeline or the Alaska–Canada Highway. Battling fierce currents and huge glacier-spawned icebergs, construction crews finished the bridge just two days before spring breakup, which would have torn away an incomplete structure.

Riverboats

Sternwheeler steamships hauled supplies and materials during construction of the Copper River and North Western Railroad, carefully navigating the winding Copper River. Unable to steam up the river past Abercrombie Rapids, the boats had to be taken apart and packed by sled and horse from Valdez, then rebuilt on the river.

Completed in 1911, the railroad created Cordova, which became a busy port whose docks were piled high with of bags of copper awaiting shipment. Chitina, an overnight stop along the rail line, grew up at the juncture of the Copper and Chitina rivers. While Kennecott was a company town, nearby McCarthy, only 6 miles away, offered a more relaxed, free-spirited community, with amenities not found in its more restrained mill-town neighbor.

The mill at Kennecott operated around the clock to meet the demand for copper during World War I, when prices were high. By the 1920s, the high-grade ore was depleted and work slowed. As copper prices fell to only five cents per pound, mining stopped. After earning more than $100 million in profits, Kennecott was abandoned in 1938, and fell into ruin. Designated a National Historic Landmark (NHL) in 1986, the mines and town site remain among the best examples of an early twentieth-century copper mining complex. The Kennecott Mines National Historic Landmark is more than just the red-and-white buildings that have become the site's icons. The history preserved at Kennecott provides glimpses into the lives of the men and women who lived and worked there; reminders of the engineers who invented the revolutionary equipment that dramatically improved the efficiency of mill operations; and the beginnings of the Kennecott Copper Corporation, one of the largest transnational copper mining companies in the world, which had its beginnings in the Kennicott Valley.

Today, Wrangell-St. Elias National Park and Preserve and the local community are interpreting the natural and cultural history of the site for those who visit the preserved remnants of the old mill's "ghost town." Park historian Geoff Bleakley notes that as early as 1925, even before mining output declined, tourists came to the

The 59-mile-long road to Kennecott and McCarthy, home of the McCarthy Lodge, follows the old Copper River and North Western Railway railroad tracks. Spikes still work their way through the gravel, especially after the Department of Transportation grades the road as part of its routine maintenance. Travelers can see historical remnants of the railroad, including old buildings and train trestles.

region—the lure of wilderness, and of copper and gold, drew adventurous spirits from all over the United States to the great northern lands.

The Park

Not long after Kennecott failed, and prior to statehood, calls to preserve the Copper River region as parkland rang out. But World War II and other events delayed the designation until 1978, when President Jimmy Carter designated Wrangell-St. Elias a national monument. Two years later, in 1980, Carter signed the Alaska National Interest Lands Conservation Act (ANILCA), creating Wrangell-St. Elias

Salmon fishing with dip nets has long been a way of life for those living in the region that is now a national park and preserve. Early dip nets were woven from spruce root.

National Park and Preserve. In total, ANILCA created ten new national parks and added lands to three already established parks. The act also designated or added land to the national wildlife refuge system, wild and scenic rivers, national conservation areas, and national forests.

Wrangell-St. Elias National Park and Preserve was established to protect huge ecosystems with diverse and dynamic natural and cultural resources as well as to honor the well-established traditions of people dependent on resources within the park. Only two gravel roads and few trails penetrate this park, which is larger than Denmark or Costa Rica, larger even than Vermont and New Hampshire combined. Some areas are designated as park, some as preserve, and within these are extensive areas reserved as wilderness. Privately owned land within the overall boundaries of the park includes land belonging to individuals, Native corporations and other entities.

Recognizing that many Alaskans live in the wilderness and find food or work in the backcountry, ANILCA established different regulations for federal lands, including wilderness areas, than exist for land outside of Alaska. For example, park visitors and local residents may use airplanes, snow machines or motorboats on the rivers to access public lands. With a permit, all-terrain vehicles may also be used in specified areas. Sport hunting and trapping are allowed in the preserve only, while sport fishing is allowed in the park and preserve. Sport hunting, trapping and fishing are subject to state harvest regulations. Residents of communities in and around the park pursue subsistence hunting, trapping and fishing in the park and preserve, with seasons and harvest limits set by the federal government.

Adventurers

Not everyone who came to this rugged land was looking for riches. Some sought the thrill of pitting themselves against its soaring peaks, and did so without the aid of global positioning devices, fleece clothing, or the safety net of airplanes that could whisk them away to safety.

- In 1897, Italian prince Luigi Amedeo Di Savoia, the Duke of Abruzzi, led a 56-day expedition to the top of Mount St. Elias via 25-mile-wide Malaspina Glacier, a route first tried—unsuccessfully—by geologist I. C. Russell. (Two previous attempts included one sponsored by the *New York Times* in 1886, led by Frederick Schwatka.)

- In 1909, Robert Dunn climbed to the top of 14,163-foot Mount Wrangell.

- The first woman to climb in Alaska, socialite Dora Keen, reached the south summit of 16,390-foot Mount Blackburn in 1912.

- By 1938, airplanes were used to support Bradford Washburn and Terris Moore in their climb to the top of 16,237-foot Mount Sanford.

Chitistone Falls, Chitistone Canyon

Subsistence harvests include fish from the rich salmon runs and moose and sheep in the park and preserve. Families gather berries and chop wood to sustain their lifestyles and to keep their cultures alive. The unique legislation that created Wrangell-St. Elias National Park and Preserve recognizes that people have been a part of the region's ecosystem for thousands of years and that the subsistence tradition is a valuable part of the park's character and significance. Because of the immense size and rugged nature of the parklands, these activities have little impact on the wilderness experience.

Subsistence living ties us closely to the land we live on.… [W]e feel a sense of pride and accomplishment in providing for our families and our communities.… For some of us, this tie to the land provides the basis for our spiritual and religious beliefs and practices. Knowing that we provided for ourselves makes the meat taste richer, the berries sweeter and the fire warmer.
　　　　　—Vicki Penwell, 2005

Nearly ten million acres, or 15,000 square miles, of Wrangell-St. Elias National Park and Preserve are managed as a wilderness area, the largest in the National Park Service system. Wilderness areas preserve the primeval character and dynamic nature of wild spaces, offering outstanding opportunities for solitude, recreation and unconfined exploration in this remote and challenging setting. Rugged terrain, the lack of established trails and treacherous river crossings make visiting the park's backcountry a world-class challenge for hikers, backpackers, campers, hunters and mountaineers. For those who accept that challenge, the rewards can be spectacular.

A vast mountain wilderness, this land of fire and ice riddled with veins of copper and gold endures the relentless power of mighty rivers that carve and sculpt on their journey to the sea. Life-giving water sets the stage for the drama that unfolds as visitors venture deep within the forests or high among the peaks to explore, looking and listening to the timeless stories whispered on the wind.

Enchanting in its remoteness, Wrangell-St. Elias National Park and Preserve is the largest jewel in this nation's treasury of national parks, one of four gems in an international World Heritage Site, truly the crown of the continent. ■

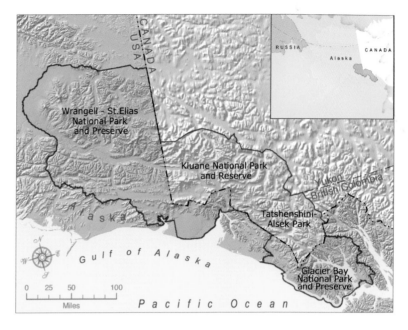

World Heritage Site

In 1979, the United Nations designated what is now Wrangell-St. Elias National Park and Preserve and its Canadian neighbor, Kluane National Park and Reserve, as an international World Heritage Site. Glacier Bay National Park and Tatshenshini-Alsek Provincial Park in British Columbia were added in 1992 and 1994, respectively.

Together, these four sites span 24 million acres and represent one of the largest internationally protected terrestrial ecosystems on Earth. While sharing World Heritage Site status, each of the four parks is managed independently within its own nation's jurisdiction.

Wrangell-St. Elias National Park and Preserve	*13 million acres*
Kluane National Park and Reserve	*5.4 million acres*
Glacier Bay National Park and Preserve	*3.3 million acres*
Tatshenshini-Alsek Provincial Park	*2.4 million acres*

Creating the Park

- **1939** Territorial Governor Ernest Gruening recommends that President Franklin D. Roosevelt set aside the area as a national monument. WWII looms and Roosevelt declines to act.

- **1958** The Statehood Act authorizes the State of Alaska to select 104 million acres from the public domain, excluding property "the right or title to which" is held by Alaska Natives.

- **1971** The Alaska Native Claims Settlement Act (ANCSA) is enacted because state selections infringe upon the holdings of Alaska Natives, who file their own land claims based on aboriginal use and occupancy.

- **1973** The Secretary of the Interior withdraws 80 million acres of the state's federally owned land in preparation for nomination for federal protection as national parks or forests.

- **1978** President Jimmy Carter invokes the 1906 Antiquities Act and establishes 17 new Alaskan national monuments, permanently protecting 56 million acres.

- **1979** Wrangell-St. Elias becomes part of an international World Heritage Site.

- **1980** Alaska National Interest Lands Conservation Act (ANILCA) is enacted and 104.5 million acres come under permanent federal protection. On December 2, President Carter signs the legislation that designates 13.2 million acres of that land as Wrangell-St. Elias National Park and Preserve.